Editor

Eric Migliaccio

Editor in Chief

Karen J. Goldfluss, M.S. Ed.

Creative Director

Sarah M. Smith

Cover Artist

Barb Lorseyedi

Art Coordinator

Renée Mc Elwee

Illustrator

Mark Mason

Imaging

James Edward Grace

Publisher

Mary D. Smith, M.S. Ed.

THE TEACHERS' PET
55 Chase Street Methuen MA 01844
978-681-0745 /www.teapet.com

NONFICTI
Reading Comp
for the Common Core

TCR 3825

CORRELATED TO COMMON CORE STANDARDS

Nonfiction and informational content-area passages

Leveled questions that encourage more in-depth thinking skills

Student-generated questions and writing activities to extend text comprehension

Connections to Common Core Informational Text Standards, Foundational Skills, and Language Standards

Teacher Created Resources

Author

Heather Wolpert-Gawron

CORRELATED TO COMMON CORE STANDARDS

For correlations to Common Core State Standards, see page 8 of this book or visit *http://www.teachercreated.com/standards/*.

Teacher Created Resources

6421 Industry Way
Westminster, CA 92683
www.teachercreated.com

ISBN: 978-1-4206-3825-7

© 2014 Teacher Created Resources
Made in U.S.A.

Teacher Created Resources

Table of Contents

Introduction

Reading and comprehending nonfiction or informational text is a challenge. Not everyone can do it well, and it needs to be specifically taught. Students who are great at reading narratives like *Lord of the Rings* or *The Princess Diaries* may still quiver at the possibility of having to understand instructions on uploading an assignment to DropBox. Students who love reading historical fiction may be fearful of reading history. Students who, with flashlight in hand, hide beneath their sheets reading the end of a science-fiction book may glaze over at the sight of an actual factual science article.

Nevertheless, informational text is all around us, and reading it well just takes working out a certain muscle — an informational-text muscle, if you will.

This book is meant to be an informational-muscle gym. Each activity is meant to build in complexity, and each activity is meant to push students in both their reading and their ability to display what they understand about what they read.

In addition to a practice passage, there are 18 reading selections contained in this book. The selections are separated into units, based on their subject matter. As a result, no matter the content area you teach, you will find applicable selections here on which your students can practice.

It doesn't matter what state you teach in, what grade level you teach, or what subject you teach; this book will aid students in understanding more deeply the difficult task of reading informational and nonfiction texts.

Reading Comprehension and the Common Core

The Common Core Standards are here, and with them come a different way to think about reading comprehension. In the past, reading informational text had been compartmentalized, each piece an isolated activity. The Common Core way of thinking is slightly different.

The goal is for students to read different genres and selections of text, pull them together in their heads, and be able to derive a theme or topic that may be shared by them all. In other words, a student may be given three different texts from three different points of view or three different genre standpoints and then have to think about their own thoughts on the subject.

Perhaps a student looks at the following:

1. Instructions on downloading an image from a digital camera
2. A biography about a famous photographer
3. A Google search history on the invention of the camera from the past to the present

Then, from those pieces, the student must pull a common theme or opinion on the topic.

Introduction *(cont.)*

Reading Comprehension and the Common Core *(cont.)*

But to be able to synthesize text (put the thoughts together), a student must first be able to read individual texts and analyze them (pull them apart). That's where this series of books comes in.

Nonfiction Reading Comprehension for the Common Core helps students to hone in on a specific piece of text, identify what's the most important concept in that piece, and answer questions about that specific selection. This will train your students for the bigger challenge that will come later in their schooling: viewing multiple texts and shaking out the meaning of them all.

If you are a public-school teacher, you may be in a state that has adopted the Common Core Standards. Use the selections in this book as individual reading-comprehension activities or pair them with similarly themed selections from other genres to give students a sense of how they will have to pull understanding from the informational, text-heavy world around us.

Copy the individual worksheets as is; or, if you are looking for a more Common Core-aligned format, mimic the Common Core multiple-choice assessments that are coming our way by entering the questions into websites that can help create computer adaptive tests (CATs).

CATs are assessments that allow a student to answer a question, which, depending on whether they answered it correctly or not, leads them to the next question that may be more geared to his or her level. In other words, each student will be taking a differentiated assessment that will end up indicating if a student is capable of answering "Novice" questions up to "Expert" questions.

There are many websites out there that can help you develop assessments to mimic those planned. Create the quiz and embed it into your class webpage or document:

Here are just a couple:

- *http://www.gotoquiz.com/create.html*
- *http://www.quibblo.com/*

Use the selections from this book, and then enter the corresponding questions into the quiz generators. We have identified questions that are higher or lower in level by assigning them a "weight" (from single-weight up through triple-weight). This weight system provides a glimpse of how hard a student should work in order to answer the question correctly. (For more information, read "Leveled Questions" on page 5.)

Regardless of how you choose to use this book, introducing students to the informational world at large is an important way to help them build skills that they will use throughout their schooling and beyond.

Introduction (cont.)

Leveled Questions

As you go through this book, you will notice that each question that students will be answering is labeled with icons that look like weights. These icons represent different levels of difficulty. The levels are based on Costa's Levels of Questioning.

The questions in this book are divided into three levels:

Level 1	Level 2	Level 3

These include sentence stems that ask students to . . .	*These include sentence stems that ask students to . . .*	*These include sentence stems that ask students to . . .*
Recite **Define** **Describe** **List**	**Infer** **Compare/Contrast** **Sequence** **Categorize**	**Judge** **Evaluate** **Create** **Hypothesize** **Predict**

The icons are a visual way to make these levels clear to students. That is important because students need to be able to recognize that some questions may require more effort and thought to answer.

Now, most of the multiple-choice questions in this book happen to fall into the Level 1 and Level 2 categories. That is pretty standard for multiple-choice questions. After all, how can asking to create something be defined by an A, B, C, or D answer? However, we may have found a way around that.

At the end of each worksheet is a place for students to develop their own questions about the material they have just read. This brings in a deeper-thinking opportunity. Having your students ask higher-level questions is a great way for assessing their comprehension of what they have read. The deeper the student's question, the deeper his or her understanding of the material.

A student handout called "The Questioning Rubric" is provided on page 6. It serves two purposes:

- It gives your students concrete examples of the elements that make up the different levels of questions.

- It gives you, the teacher, a way to determine whether a student-generated question is a low- or high-level inquiry.

The goal of a student is to ask more challenging questions of oneself. The goal of the teacher is to be able to track better the level of production for each student. This book helps do both.

Introduction *(cont.)*

The Questioning Rubric

Answering questions is one way of proving you understand a reading selection. However, creating your very own questions about the selection might be an even better way. Developing thoughtful, high-level questions can really display your understanding of what you have read, and it also makes other students think about the reading passage in a unique way.

So what types of questions can you ask? There are three levels of questions, and for each one there is a different amount of work your brain must do to answer the question. We've chosen to use a symbol of a weight in order to represent this amount. Consult this chart when thinking about what defines a great question as compared to a so-so one.

Icon	Description
	A single weight represents a **Level 1** question that doesn't require much brainpower to answer correctly. The question only asks readers to tell what they know about the selection. For example, any inquiry that asks for a simple "Yes or No" or "True or False" response is a Level 1 question.
	A double weight represents a **Level 2** question that requires you to use a little more brain sweat. (Ewww!) This question asks readers to think a little beyond the passage. It may require some analysis, inference, or interpretation. Questions involving comparing/contrasting or sequencing often fall here.
	A **Level 3** question really makes you work for its answer. These questions allow you to show off your knowledge of a topic by asking you to create, wonder, judge, evaluate, and/or apply what you know to what you think. These types of questions are much more open-ended than Level 1 or Level 2 questions.

Don't be scared to sweat a little in answering or developing Level 3 questions. Working out your brain in this way will help prepare you for some heavy lifting later on in life. So as you progress through this book, use this rubric as a resource to make sure your questions are as high-level as possible.

Need help getting started? The following sentence stems will give you ideas about how to create questions for each level.

Level 1
- Write the definition of…
- Describe how _____ is…
- List the details that go into…

Level 2
- What can you infer from _____?
- Compare _____ with _____.
- Contrast _____ with _____.
- Write the steps in sequence from _____.
- Place _____ in the right category.

Level 3
- How would you judge the _____?
- How would you evaluate the _____?
- How can you create a _____?
- Hypothesize what would happen if _____.
- What do you predict will happen in _____?

Introduction *(cont.)*

Achievement Graph

As you correct your responses in this book, track how well you improve. Calculate how many answers you got right after each worksheet and mark your progress here based on the number of weights each question was worth. For instance, if you get the first problem correct and it is worth two weights, then write "2" in the first column. Do this for each column and add up your total at the end.

Reading Passage	1	2	3	4	Total
"What Is a Geode?"					
"One Final Flight"					
"An Eye for Color"					
"The Magical Möbius Strip"					
"The Five Most Deadly Sharks"					
"Unsung Heroes"					
"Hamilton vs. Burr"					
"A New Kind of Treasure Hunt"					
"Record-Breaking Mountains"					
"A Famous Face"					
"The Blue Jean King"					
"Mario Batali"					
"Laura Ingalls Wilder"					
"The Superpowers of Stan Lee"					
"Worth the Risk?"					
"Selling Made Easy"					
"E-mailing Etiquette"					
"Translating Thoughts Into Words"					
"Speaking Without Fear"					

Common Core State Standards

The lessons and activities included in *Nonfiction Reading Comprehension for the Common Core, Grade 4* meet the following Common Core State Standards. (©Copyright 2010. National Governors Association Center for Best Practices and Council of Chief State School Officers. All right reserved.) For more information about the Common Core State Standards, go to *http://www.corestandards.org/* or visit *http://www.teachercreated.com/standards/*.

Informational Text Standards	
Key Ideas and Details	**Pages**
CCSS.ELA.RI.4.1. Refer to details and examples in a text when explaining what the text says explicitly and when drawing inferences from the text.	10–47
Craft and Structure	**Pages**
CCSS.ELA.RI.4.4. Determine the meaning of general academic and domain-specific words or phrases in a text relevant to a grade 4 topic or subject area.	10–47
Range of Reading and Level of Text Complexity	**Pages**
CCSS.ELA.RI.4.10. By the end of year, read and comprehend informational texts, including history/social studies, science, and technical texts, in the grades 4–5 text complexity band proficiently, with scaffolding as needed at the high end of the range.	10–47
Foundational Skills Standards	
Phonics and Word Recognition	**Pages**
CCSS.ELA.RF.4.3. Know and apply grade-level phonics and word-analysis skills in decoding words.	10–47
Fluency	**Pages**
CCSS.ELA.RF.4.4. Read with sufficient accuracy and fluency to support comprehension.	10–47
Language Standards	
Conventions of Standard English	**Pages**
CCSS.ELA.L.4.1. Demonstrate command of the conventions of standard English grammar and usage when writing or speaking.	11–47
CCSS.ELA.L.4.2. Demonstrate command of the conventions of standard English capitalization, punctuation, and spelling when writing.	11–47
Knowledge of Language	**Pages**
CCSS.ELA.L.4.3. Use knowledge of language and its conventions when writing, speaking, reading, or listening.	10–47
Vocabulary Acquisition and Use	**Pages**
CCSS.ELA.L.4.4. Determine or clarify the meaning of unknown and multiple-meaning words and phrases based on *grade 4 reading and content*, choosing flexibly from an array of strategies.	10–47
CCSS.ELA.L.4.5. Demonstrate understanding of figurative language, word relationships, and nuances in word meanings.	10–47
Writing Standards	
Research to Build and Present Knowledge	**Pages**
CCSS.ELA.L.4.9. Draw evidence from literary or informational texts to support analysis, reflection, and research.	11–47

Multiple-Choice Test-Taking Tips

Some multiple-choice questions are straightforward and easy. "I know the answer!" your brain yells right away. Some questions, however, stump even the most prepared student. In cases like that, you have to make an educated guess. An educated guess is a guess that uses what you know to help guide your attempt. You don't put your hand over your eyes and pick a random letter! You select it because you've thought about the format of the question, the word choice, the other possible answers, and the language of what's being asked. By making an educated guess, you're increasing your chances of guessing correctly. Whenever you are taking a multiple-choice assessment, you should remember to follow the rules below:

1. Read the directions. It's crucial. You may assume you know what is being asked, but sometimes directions can be tricky when you least expect them to be.

2. Read the questions before you read the passage. Doing this allows you to read the text through a more educated and focused lens. For example, if you know that you will be asked to identify the main idea, you can be on the lookout for that ahead of time.

3. Don't skip a question. Instead, try to make an educated guess. That starts with crossing off the ones you definitely know are not the correct answer. For instance, if you have four possible answers (A, B, C, D) and you can cross off two of them immediately, you've doubled your chances of guessing correctly. If you don't cross off any obvious ones, you would only have a 25% chance of guessing right. However, if you cross off two, you now have a 50% chance!

4. Read carefully for words like *always*, *never*, *not*, *except*, and *every*. Words like these are there to make you stumble. They make the question very specific. Sometimes an answer can be right some of the time, but if a word like *always* or *every* is in the question, the answer must be right *all of the time.*

5. After reading a question, try to come up with the answer first in your head before looking at the possible answers. That way, you will be less likely to bubble or click something you aren't sure about.

6. In questions with an "All of the Above" answer, think of it this way: if you can identify at least two that are correct, then "All of the Above" is probably the correct answer.

7. In questions with a "None of the Above" answer, think of it this way: if you can identify at least two that are *not* correct, then "None of the Above" is probably the correct answer.

8. Don't keep changing your answer. Unless you are sure you made a mistake, usually the first answer you chose is the right one.

What Is a Geode?

A geode is a beautiful rock formation that gives you a peek inside a natural wonder. *Geo* means "earth," and a geode is a small piece of earth. Geodes are round or oval in shape. They are plain and dull on the outside but full of sparkling crystals on the inside. If you find a geode, you know that you are looking at a piece of Earth's history.

It takes a long time for a geode to form. They are formed in rounded areas like those made from the gas bubbles in volcanic rock. Over a long period of time, minerals leak into the hollow formed by the gas bubble. The mineral hardens into a crusty shell while it continues to form on the inside of what will be the geode. It can take hundreds of millions of years for a geode to actually fill in the round shape. This is why most geodes that we find today are still hollow. The crystal formations create an inside layer of beauty within the outer shell.

Many geodes have crystals on the inside that are white or even purple in color. Most are made from quartz, but some can be made from amethyst. The crystal formations form hundreds of sparkly facets. A facet is a flat surface that can reflect light and be very smooth to the touch.

Geodes can be found in many desert areas, but they have been discovered all over the world. While many American states are known for their geodes, only Iowa has named the geode its official state rock.

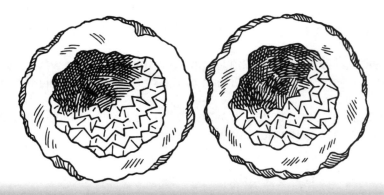

Answer the following questions about the story "What Is a Geode?" The weights show you how hard you will need to work to find each answer.

1. What does the prefix *geo-* mean?

    Ⓐ go

    Ⓑ maps

    Ⓒ earth

    Ⓓ rocky

2. According to the passage, what kind of rocks have formed geodes?

    Ⓐ volcanic

    Ⓑ quartz

    Ⓒ concrete

    Ⓓ gravel

3. According to the description in the passage, what does a facet feel like?

    Ⓐ spiky

    Ⓑ sharp

    Ⓒ puffy

    Ⓓ smooth

4. According to the story, where is a location in which you would most likely find a geode?

    Ⓐ Antarctica

    Ⓑ a rainforest

    Ⓒ the Sahara desert

    Ⓓ the Pacific Ocean

On the lines below, write your own question based on "What Is a Geode?" Circle the correct picture on the left to show the level of the question you wrote.

_____

_____

_____

_____

On a separate piece of paper . . .

- Write a sentence that includes the word *reflect*.

- Write a short story about finding a huge round rock in your backyard. Imagine you take a hammer and crack the rock open. Describe what you find inside.

One Final Flight

Liftoff! On May 16, 2011, the space shuttle *Endeavour* launched into space for the last time. The rocket boosters separated as planned. Then, the engines shut down so that the fuel tank could then be discarded. (The word *discarded* means "tossed away.") All of this had to happen in order for *Endeavour* to begin its final journey into space. After this adventure, it was to be retired. That is, the space shuttle program would soon be over. *Endeavour's* final journey into space marked the final shuttle launch for the final mission of the program.

The astronauts in the shuttle set their alarms for their first morning on the job. They woke up to a famous song from the band U2 called "Beautiful Day." Their first job was to look at the heat shield to make sure there was no damage during the launch. Then, they got ready to dock with the International Space Station (ISS). The ISS is a scientific lab that floats around in space. It was built by many countries. *Endeavour's* crew brought some spare parts to the space station. After all, the astronauts working on the ISS can't just go to the local hardware store! Supplies need to be brought to them.

On this final journey into space, the astronauts took four space walks. Each lasted around six hours. They also helped set up a huge antenna to the ISS.

There was one scary moment while the astronauts were working in space. A warning alarm went off in the crew's sleeping quarters. However, it was a false alarm. A plastic bag had floated into the room and got stuck in a fan. Whew!

On June 1, 2011, the *Endeavour* landed safely for the 25th and last time. However, it had one final journey to make. This time, *Endeavour* was slowly towed through the streets of Los Angeles to end its final journey at the California Science Museum. You can see it parked there today.

Answer the following questions about the story "One Final Flight." The weights show you how hard you will need to work to find each answer.

1. According to the article, why is the ISS called the International Space Station?

Ⓐ It was built by many countries.

Ⓑ It serves many different kinds of food.

Ⓒ It is a rocket ship with captains from different countries.

Ⓓ It monitors all countries on Earth.

2. About how many **total** hours did *Endeavour's* astronauts walk in space during their final journey?

Ⓐ 4   Ⓒ 16

Ⓑ 6   Ⓓ 24

3. How many flights did the *Endeavour* take?

Ⓐ 21   Ⓒ 23

Ⓑ 22   Ⓓ 25

4. What does the word *discarded* mean?

Ⓐ "tossed away"   Ⓒ "insulted"

Ⓑ "played with cards" Ⓓ "locked up"

On the lines below, write your own question based on "One Final Flight." Circle the correct picture on the left to show the level of the question you wrote.

_____

_____

_____

_____

_____

_____

On a separate piece of paper . . .

• Write a sentence that includes the word *launch*.

• Imagine you are on your last mission as an astronaut. What would you most like to see? Why?

An Eye for Color

Imagine an interspecies contest to find out who sees the most colors. Since the contest is *interspecies*, it would involve every kind of species possible. So which species do you believe sees the most colors? If you guessed humans, you would be wrong. It's not us. Humans see only three pure colors. For instance, we see red and blue. However, we also see the many combinations of red and blue. Other animals see even better than humans. For instance, the butterfly sees many more pure colors than we do.

However, the animal that sees the most color is the little known mantis shrimp. It can see 16 pure colors! Just think of the combinations! Actually, it's impossible to think of them. We cannot think about those colors because we have never seen them.

The mantis shrimp lives in the ocean. Like many shrimp-like creatures, their bodies are jointed in different segments. They have three pairs of legs on which to walk. They also have four pairs of claws, including a big set in the front that are folded like those of a praying mantis. Their big claws can punch so quickly that they move 50 times faster then the human eye can blink. Despite their interesting claws, however, it's their eyes that are really unique.

Nobody knows why the mantis shrimp adapted to see so many colors. Why did they change over many years so that they could see so many colors? Scientists think they adapted to catch their food. For a mantis shrimp, its food glows with extraterrestrial colors. That means the food glows with colors that seem out of this world! Glowing food is easier to catch for the mantis shrimp. Just imagine the colorful world these little creatures live in!

Answer the following questions about the story "An Eye for Color." The weights show you how hard you will need to work to find each answer.

1. How many pure colors does a human see?

Ⓐ 4   Ⓒ 16
Ⓑ 3   Ⓓ 10

2. What does *adapted* mean?

Ⓐ "changed over time"   Ⓒ "built"
Ⓑ "stayed the same"   Ⓓ "destroyed"

3. How many total legs does a mantis shrimp have?

Ⓐ 2   Ⓒ 4
Ⓑ 3   Ⓓ 6

4. According to the passage, how fast does the mantis shrimp punch?

Ⓐ faster than a human blinks
Ⓑ faster than a cheetah runs
Ⓒ faster than a butterfly travels
Ⓓ faster than a locomotive

On the lines below, write your own question based on "An Eye for Color." Circle the correct picture on the left to show the level of the question you wrote.

_____

_____

_____

_____

On a separate piece of paper . . .

- Write a sentence that includes the word *extraterrestrial*.

- Pretend that you are the first person to see a new color for the first time. Try to describe the color to another student.

The Magical Möbius Strip

A Möbius strip is a twisted, two-dimensional surface that has no beginning and no end. How is that possible, you might ask? Well, let's look at a small Möbius strip so that you can visualize this advanced mathematical subject.

Below is a drawing of a Möbius strip. Picture yourself starting to walk around

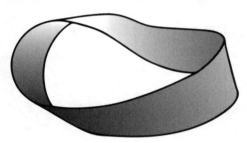

the inside of that strip. Eventually, if you trace your path with your eye, you'll see that you actually transverse both sides of the loop. The word *transverse* uses the prefix *trans–*. That can mean "to travel across or through something."

The first Möbius strip was created in 1858. It was created by two German mathematicians. There names were August Ferdinand Möbius and Johann Benedict Listing. It looks like it might be difficult to make, but it's actually very simple to create your own Möbius strip.

Step 1: Take a long strip of paper.

Step 2: Give it a half-twist.

Step 3: Tape the two ends together.

Now, starting on one spot on the paper, use your pencil to draw a continuous line, a line that never stops, all around the strip. You'll find that your pencil lands back at the point where it started. By creating your own Möbius strip, you'll discover that it's amazing. There is no "outside" and "inside." There is only one side.

This isn't magic. It's math!

Answer the following questions about the story "The Magical Möbius Strip." The weights show you how hard you will need to work to find each answer.

1. A Möbius strip is an example of

  Ⓐ science.   Ⓒ English.

  Ⓑ history.   Ⓓ math.

2. How many sides does a Möbius strip have?

  Ⓐ 6   Ⓒ 1

  Ⓑ 3   Ⓓ 2

3. Based on the definition of the prefix *trans–*, what can you assume the word *transmit* means?

  Ⓐ "to catch"   Ⓒ "to find"

  Ⓑ "to leave"   Ⓓ "to send"

4. When was the first Möbius strip created?

  Ⓐ 1858   Ⓒ 1885

  Ⓑ 1585   Ⓓ 1558

On the lines below, write your own question based on "The Magical Möbius Strip." Circle the correct picture on the left to show the level of the question you wrote.

_____

_____

_____

_____

On a separate piece of paper . . .

- Write a sentence that includes the word *continuous*.
- Create your own Möbius strip. Try to write a sentence on it that ends exactly where it begins!

The Five Most Deadly Sharks

What is it about sharks that humans find so frightening? Is it the teeth? Perhaps it is the fact that they are rulers of an underwater kingdom that we have yet to conquer? People have long been fascinated and freaked out by these predators of the seas.

For example, many of us imagine that sharks are human-hunting villains of the oceans. Does this terrifying image give an accurate picture of these creatures? It really doesn't. The fact is, there are over 370 species of sharks. Only about a dozen of them could even **pose** a threat to humans.

Let's look at the top five scariest sharks:

5. Sand Tiger Shark

4. Requiem Shark

3. Bull Shark

2. Tiger Shark

1. Great White Shark

It's important to know that over half of all attacks are only from numbers 1–3 on the list. Of those three, the great white is the most dangerous by far. It accounts for more attacks than the bull shark and tiger shark combined.

So why do sharks attack us? Many scientists believe that most shark attacks are, in fact, accidental. Sharks don't want to hurt people. They really don't want to eat us at all. Maybe we don't taste good. Maybe we're just too much trouble. Generally, scientists believe, sharks get confused. They think we are one of their favorite dinners: the seal.

Answer the following questions about the story "The Five Most Deadly Sharks." The weights show you how hard you will need to work to find each answer.

1. According to the article, how many species of sharks could be dangerous to humans?
- Ⓐ 18
- Ⓑ 12
- Ⓒ 20
- Ⓓ 25

2. What is the most dangerous shark by far?
- Ⓐ the bull shark
- Ⓑ the tiger shark
- Ⓒ the great white shark
- Ⓓ the requiem shark

3. According to the article, what is one of the favorite meals for a shark?
- Ⓐ humans
- Ⓑ fish
- Ⓒ other sharks
- Ⓓ seals

4. Based on the passage, what can you infer is the meaning of the word *pose*?
- Ⓐ present
- Ⓑ dismiss
- Ⓒ reject
- Ⓓ move

On the lines below, write your own question based on "The Five Most Deadly Sharks." Circle the correct picture on the left to show the level of the question you wrote.

_____

_____

_____

_____

On a separate piece of paper . . .

- Write a sentence that includes the word *species*.

- Sharks have evolved to become very efficient hunters. Create a list of adaptations that you feel make the shark such a successful predator.

Unsung Heroes

The carrier pigeon is an unsung hero. That is, it is an animal that is often forgotten about and rarely given the credit it deserves. Carrier pigeons look like ordinary birds, ones that you might see at the park. However, they have a secret ability. Carrier pigeons can be trained to carry messages across great distances (up to about 100 miles). Then, it can come straight home to its roost.

Carrier pigeons were once used a lot. Before radio, these birds could help people quickly communicate. They were used to send messages and small items from one location to another. During the 19th century, they were used to send messages from a besieged city to allies outside of the walls of the town. A besieged city is one that is surrounded by an enemy. Years later, hospitals used carrier pigeons to transport small vials of medicine between them. Carrier pigeons were also used during World War I and World War II. They sent messages between the battlefield and the home base.

Training a carrier pigeon required teaching the bird where home was and where food could be found. Home was where the pigeon always returned. Food was kept in the location where the pigeon needed to go. If those two points remained fixed, the bird could learn to travel between them very reliably.

Life for a carrier pigeon was not all food and sleep, however. It could be very dangerous. On battlefields, the enemy would send hawks to hunt them down. Enemy soldiers were often on the lookout to shoot down the birds.

Some remote areas of the world still keep small troops of carrier pigeons. These areas are very isolated. However, this is a rare practice these days. The talents of carrier pigeons have been made unnecessary by a much faster way to send messages, the Internet.

Answer the following questions about the story "Unsung Heroes." The weights show you how hard you will need to work to find each answer.

1. Based on the passage, what is the maximum distance a carrier pigeon can travel?
   - (A) about 100 feet
   - (B) about 200 miles
   - (C) about 19 miles
   - (D) about 100 miles

2. How were the carrier pigeons used?
   - (A) to fly around parks
   - (B) to transport small items and messages
   - (C) for a hobby
   - (D) to walk between hospitals

3. According to the article, what factors have made the usage of carrier pigeons unnecessary?
   - (A) hawks
   - (B) soldiers
   - (C) the Internet
   - (D) all of the above

4. What can you infer is the best meaning of the word *allies*?
   - (A) enemies
   - (B) friends
   - (C) peasants
   - (D) soldiers

On the lines below, write your own question based on "Unsung Heroes." Circle the correct picture on the left to show the level of the question you wrote.

_____

_____

_____

_____

_____

On a separate piece of paper . . .

- Write a sentence that includes the word *communicate*.

- Pretend you live in the 19th century, and your town is under siege. Write a short letter in which you ask for help from an ally.

Hamilton vs. Burr

Politicians are always debating. They argue frequently, and often it is loud. While they may disagree, no harm usually comes from these debates. No one is ever in real danger. However, that can't be said for a debate from long ago in U.S. history. This debate took place between Alexander Hamilton and Aaron Burr. After years of arguing, these two had an infamous duel. It ended in disaster for them both.

Alexander Hamilton and Aaron Burr were two American politicians. Hamilton was the secretary of the treasury. Aaron Burr served as vice president during Thomas Jefferson's first term of office.

It's a fact that the two men did not like each other. They disagreed about politics. They disagreed personally, as well. This dislike lasted for years. They let it build up to a point where they felt they could no longer avoid a fight. On July 11, 1804, the two men met to duel. This duel was not with swords, but with pistols. In the end, Burr killed Hamilton.

There is a debate about this historical mystery. It was tradition to show up at a duel and actually shoot at the ground or away. This showed courage because the person showed up to the duel, but didn't hurt anyone. People knew Hamilton was against dueling. Historians believe that he actually shot his pistol at a tree without the intention of hurting Burr. Was this an accident, or was he really a bad aim? Meanwhile, Burr's bullet hit Hamilton. However, some believe Burr may have been aiming away from Hamilton and accidentally hit him. Nobody knows for sure.

Years later, Burr seemed to show regret about fighting. He stated that if he had read more peaceful writers, "I should have known the world was wide enough for Hamilton and me."

The event was not just the end of the secretary of the treasury. It was also the end of Burr's political career. The public didn't approve anymore of handling disagreements in such a violent way. As a result, an anti-dueling law was soon passed.

Name: _____

Answer the following questions about the story "Hamilton vs. Burr." The weights show you how hard you will need to work to find each answer.

1. Based on the passage, what can you guess is the meaning of the word *infamous*?

Ⓐ "really well known"   Ⓒ "not famous"
Ⓑ "forgettable"   Ⓓ "known by a few people"

2. Alexander Hamilton was the _____.

Ⓐ president   Ⓒ vice president
Ⓑ secretary of state   Ⓓ secretary of the treasury

3. During which season was their infamous duel?

Ⓐ summer   Ⓒ spring
Ⓑ fall   Ⓓ winter

4. Why is the duel still considered a mystery in history?

Ⓐ Nobody knows how Hamilton died.
Ⓑ Nobody knows when the duel happened.
Ⓒ People don't know if the two meant to fight to the death.
Ⓓ Nobody knows where Aaron Burr ran to after the duel.

On the lines below, write your own question based on "Hamilton vs. Burr." Circle the correct picture on the left to show the level of the question you wrote.

_____

_____

_____

On a separate piece of paper . . .

- Write a sentence that includes the word *regret*.
- Think about an argument that you have had. How did you handle the disagreement? How do you move on from an argument?

A New Kind of Treasure Hunt

Have you ever gone on a scavenger hunt? This is a type of game in which clues lead you from one location to the next in a search for treasure. Now, there is a new kind of scavenger hunt that could only be from the 21st century. It uses technology, and it is called *geocaching*.

What is geocaching? Well, as the prefix *geo-* indicates, it has to do with the earth. The other part of the word, *cache*, is actually a French word. It means a temporary location to hide something. Geocaching combines the two, and describes this new kind of game. Geocaching is an outdoor scavenger hunt that anyone can play.

The object of this game is to use a GPS (Global Positioning System) to find clues. You may have seen a GPS in a car. It helps to give directions and find locations. In this game, a GPS will lead you to a hidden container that has been planted in a specific location. Once you find the object, you replace it so that another participant can follow clues to the same location. Then, you share stories and photos online about your adventure as you track down the hidden object.

The objects can be found anywhere. You may be led to a park or perhaps to a nearby lake. You never know where objects have been hidden and logged.

There are different websites that help you join the game. These websites register different locations and objects. Your parent or guardian enters a zip code. (Always ask a parent or guardian before sharing any of your information online.) Next, you use a GPS to help find the nearest treasure.

Geocaching is a fun game that can happen all over the world. So, whether you are looking for something to do this weekend or something to do while on vacation, perhaps there's a hidden cache just waiting to be found near you. Well, what are you waiting for? On your marks, get set, go!

Answer the following questions about the story "A New Kind of Treasure Hunt." The weights show you how hard you will need to work to find each answer.

1. What does "GPS" stand for?

Ⓐ "Geo Placement System"

Ⓑ "Global Positioning System"

Ⓒ "Geography Positive Security"

Ⓓ "Global Placement Situation"

2. According to the article, why do you replace the object that you find?

Ⓐ because it costs money to supply the objects

Ⓑ so others can find your clues

Ⓒ so other participants have something to find

Ⓓ so they can add to the treasure with their own

3. What is the purpose of a GPS?

Ⓐ finding locations   Ⓒ keeping Earth clean

Ⓑ making driving easier   Ⓓ finding your lost items

4. Based on what you learned in the article, what might the word *geography* mean?

Ⓐ the study of locations   Ⓒ the study of gases

Ⓑ the study of shapes   Ⓓ the study of Earth

On the lines below, write your own question based on "A New Kind of Treasure Hunt." Circle the correct picture on the left to show the level of the question you wrote.

_____

_____

_____

_____

On a separate piece of paper . . .

• Write a sentence that includes the word *temporary*.

• Where would you bury a treasure? Draw a map leading from your school desk to the treasure that you might one day hide.

Record-Breaking Mountains

There are many huge mountains in the world. Some are really tall. Others are really long. Others are very wide. Each is unique. Mountains appear on every continent. Let's look at which mountain ranges are the record breakers.

- **Highest Altitude** — Mt. Everest is in Asia. It is considered the tallest mountain in the world. In reality, it's the highest in altitude. It is the tallest mountain from sea level to its peak. The term "sea level" means at the level the ocean's surface begins. So from the surface of the sea to the top of the mountain, Mt. Everest scores the highest. It is about 29,000 feet above sea level.

- **Tallest Mountain** — If we count the base of the mountain to the peak of the mountain, then the tallest mountain is Mauna Kea. Mauna Kea is an island in the Pacific Ocean. Therefore, we can say that its base is the ocean floor itself. This makes this mountain about 33,000 feet tall.

- **Longest Mountain Range** — The longest range is not actually found on land. It's found underwater. It's called the mid-ocean ridge. It's over 40,000 miles long!

Earth's mountain ranges form a lot of the character on the surface of our planet. What would our planet look like without them?

Answer the following questions about the story "Record-Breaking Mountains." The weights show you how hard you will need to work to find each answer.

1. Which mountain has the highest altitude?

(A) Mt. Olympus
(B) The Andes
(C) Mt. Everest
(D) Mauna Kea

2. According to the article, what is Mauna Kea?

(A) a plateau
(B) an ocean
(C) an island
(D) a mid-ocean ridge

3. How long is the mid-ocean ridge?

(A) 40 miles
(B) 400 miles
(C) 4000 miles
(D) 40,000 miles

4. From the information given in the story, you can infer that the peak of Mauna Kea rises _____ above sea level.

(A) less than 29,000 feet
(B) more than 29,000 feet
(C) about 33,000 feet
(D) almost 40,000 miles

On the lines below, write your own question based on "Record-Breaking Mountains." Circle the correct picture on the left to show the level of the question you wrote.

_____

_____

_____

_____

On a separate piece of paper . . .

- Write a sentence that includes the word *surface*.

- Let's say you are packing for a trip to hike Mt. Everest. You can only take things that you can fit into one backpack. Make a list of the important items that you would need for such a trip.

A Famous Face

There have been over 40 presidents in the history of the United States. Few made as big of an impact on the country as Abraham Lincoln. His strength and character led the U.S. through one of its toughest times. Lincoln is also one of the U.S.'s most recognizable presidents. Many Americans can identify him immediately. For many, it is Lincoln's beard that makes his face so memorable. It is hard to picture Lincoln without his moustache-less beard. However, if it were not for an 11-year-old girl, we might have a very different image of Lincoln. If it were not for Grace Bedell, Abraham Lincoln might never have grown a beard.

Grace's father believed in Lincoln. He wanted him to be president. One day he brought home a picture of Lincoln and showed it to his 11-year-old daughter, Grace. She did not like the look of Lincoln's beardless face. She found it too thin and not very attractive. She said to her mother, "He would look better if he wore whiskers, and I mean to write and tell him so."

On October 15, 1860, Grace mailed a letter to Lincoln. She sent it from her home in Westfield, New York. In it, she talked about her four brothers and her baby sister and how, "if I was a man I would vote for you." She also asked him to grow a beard. She wrote, "All the ladies like whiskers and they would tease their husbands to vote for you and then you would be President." Lincoln received her letter. On October 19, 1860, he wrote back. In his letter, he stated that he had never worn whiskers and he asked, "do you not think people would call it a silly affection if I were to begin it now?"

Despite Lincoln's question to Grace, he did begin to grow his whiskers. By the time he was sworn in as president in February of 1861, Lincoln had a full growth of beard along his jawline. It was at that time that Lincoln stopped in Grace's hometown with the hopes of seeing her. Several years later, Grace Bedell recalled what Abraham Lincoln said to her that day. "Gracie, " he said, "look at my whiskers. I have been growing them for you."

Answer the following questions about the story "A Famous Face." The weights show you how hard you will need to work to find each answer.

1. According to the passage, what is a synonym for the word *recognizable*?

Ⓐ facial   Ⓑ memorable   Ⓒ attractive   Ⓓ presidential

2. In his letter to Grace, what seems to be Lincoln's thoughts about growing a beard?

Ⓐ He thinks it's a fantastic idea, and he'll start growing one immediately.
Ⓑ He's concerned that people will think he's trying to be someone he's not.
Ⓒ He's worried that a beard would look terrible on him, so he won't grow one.
Ⓓ He says he once had a beard, and he has been thinking about growing one again.

3. About how much time passed from when Grace wrote to Lincoln to when he wrote back?

Ⓐ about 11 years   Ⓒ about 4 months
Ⓑ about 14 days   Ⓓ about 4 days

4. Which of these pieces of information can you infer from the story?

Ⓐ Everyone in Westfield voted for Abraham Lincoln in 1860.
Ⓑ Grace Bedell was not impressed by Lincoln's beard once she saw it.
Ⓒ Grace insisted that Lincoln visited her after he won the election.
Ⓓ Women could not vote in the presidential election of 1860.

On the lines below, write your own question based on "A Famous Face." Circle the correct picture on the left to show the level of the question you wrote.

_____

_____

_____

_____

On a separate piece of paper . . .

- Write a sentence that includes the word *recognizable*.

- Picture a famous person who is very recognizable. You can choose someone from the past or present. Name this person and tell what about his or her appearance is so recognizable.

The Blue Jean King

Jeans are comfortable. Jeans are long-lasting. It's possible that no matter where you are, if you are in a group of people, someone is wearing a pair of jeans. Who was the mastermind behind one of the most well known clothing items? His name was Levi Strauss.

Levi was born in 1829 in Germany. His family was Jewish, and they experienced a lot of discrimination. They were treated unfairly because of who they were. Levi's father died when his son was 6 years old. His mother packed up the family, and they made the long journey to the United States. They settled in New York City.

In the late 1840s, the California Gold Rush exploded. People went crazy. Many people traveled to California to find treasure of their own. Even Levi joined the rush, selling goods to the miners. He sold small items and different fabrics. Miners needed fabrics because working with rocks and dirt is hard work. Their pants always got holes in them.

Then, in 1872, one of Strauss' customers approached him with an idea. The man had invented a new way to make some pants that could endure the dirt and grime of being a miner. Strauss paid for the patent for the new pants. He became a part owner of the idea. A patent is a document that proves you were the first to invent something. The pants were unique because they used metal rivets. This made them last longer. They were eventually dyed dark blue to hide stains, as well.

Eventually, the demand for Levi Strauss' new pants was so great that he had to build a factory to make them. To this day, Levi's blue jeans are worn around the world. Do you have a pair or two in your closet?

Answer the following questions about the story "The Blue Jean King." The weights show you how hard you will need to work to find each answer.

1. Based on the passage, what can you determine the word *endure* means?

    Ⓐ live through   Ⓒ become bored

    Ⓑ recycle   Ⓓ collapse

2. About how old was Strauss when he was approached by a customer with a new invention?

    Ⓐ 29   Ⓑ 33   Ⓒ 43   Ⓓ 53

3. From the story, we know that Strauss moved from

    Ⓐ Germany to New York to California.

    Ⓑ New York to California to Germany.

    Ⓒ Germany to England to New York.

    Ⓓ California to New York to Germany.

4. Based on the information in the passage, what can be said about Levi Strauss?

    Ⓐ He hated traveling.   Ⓒ He only did what was familiar to him.

    Ⓑ He never took risks.   Ⓓ He took many chances that paid off.

On the lines below, write your own question based on "The Blue Jean King." Circle the correct picture on the left to show the level of the question you wrote.

_____

_____

_____

_____

_____

On a separate piece of paper . . .

- Write a sentence that includes the word *discrimination*.

- Some people have a favorite pair of jeans, something they can just slip into and feel comfortable. What is your most comfortable item of clothing, and how does wearing it make you feel?

Mario Batali

What do you like on your pizza? Cheese? Pepperoni? How about squash blossoms and chilies? That's one pizza that is served at Mario Batali's restaurants.

Mario Batali is a chef and restaurant owner. He specializes in preparing unique Italian food. He has written books and starred in many TV shows. He likes teaching people about high-quality food.

Mario is an expert on the history of Italian food. He is also an expert at its regional cuisine. This means that he knows a lot about the foods served in the little areas all around Italy. One dish that is famous in Rome may not be famous in Venice. A dish that is famous in Tuscany may not be as famous in Florence. Mario knows them all. He knows where they are from and how they were created.

Mario Batali was born in Seattle, Washington, but many members of his family came from Italy. As a young man, Mario attended a famous cooking school called Le Cordon Bleu. However, he didn't stay long. He believed that to really learn to cook, he needed to be in a working kitchen, not a classroom. He began working at a restaurant in New York as a dishwasher. He was promoted to pizza maker. Finally, he began assisting executive chefs until he became one himself. Eventually, he moved to Italy and became an apprentice, or worker-in-training. He learned more about authentic Italian cooking.

Mario opened up his first restaurant in the early 1990s. From there, his food took off! He now has restaurants all over the world, from America to Singapore. He became a real celebrity when he joined The Food Network. Everyone who wanted to learn Italian cooking could watch him on TV. He taught cooking with a smile.

Even after all of his success, Mario never lost sight of what was important: good food. The Mario Batali Foundation helps to educate children, not only about food, but also about themselves.

Answer the following questions about the story "Mario Batali." The weights show you how hard you will need to work to find each answer.

1. Mario Batali is an expert in foods found in what country?

   Ⓐ Germany   Ⓒ Singapore

   Ⓑ America   Ⓓ Italy

2. According to the article, why did Mario Batali leave cooking school?

   Ⓐ He failed to get good grades.

   Ⓑ He wanted to learn in a real restaurant.

   Ⓒ He didn't get along with his teachers.

   Ⓓ He couldn't pay the tuition.

3. Based on the information given in this article, which of these cities is not in Italy?

   Ⓐ Venice   Ⓒ Seattle

   Ⓑ Tuscany   Ⓓ Florence

4. What can you infer is the meaning of the phrase "took off" as used in the article?

   Ⓐ traveled   Ⓒ became really popular

   Ⓑ ran away   Ⓓ left Batali behind

On the lines below, write your own question based on "Mario Batali." Circle the correct picture on the left to show the level of the question you wrote.

_____

_____

_____

_____

_____

On a separate piece of paper . . .

- Write a sentence that includes the word *promoted*.

- If you could invent a kind of pizza, what would it be? What toppings would you use?

Laura Ingalls Wilder

Laura Ingalls Wilder was born in 1869 in Wisconsin. She was born in a log cabin to Charles and Caroline Ingalls. Two years later, her family traveled across the prairies to Kansas. From there, her family moved many times to many different towns in the Midwest. This was due to many reasons. Perhaps the crops failed or there was work elsewhere. It was a hard life, but it was one in which her family stayed strong and were there for each other.

She and her three siblings attended school when they could. But they generally taught themselves because they moved around so much. Nevertheless, Laura Ingalls Wilder wanted to become a teacher. At 15, she accomplished her goal. She began working in a one-room schoolhouse miles from home. She lived with a local family. This was common for teachers who worked in schools far from towns and cities.

In 1885, Ingalls married Alonzo Wilder. Eventually they started a farmhouse in Missouri. There, they raised their family and lived quietly for many years.

Then in 1910, Rose Ingalls, their daughter, suggested that her mom write about her childhood on the prairies. It took until 1932, but finally the *Little House* series was born. The first one was called *Little House in the Big Woods*. It is set in a log cabin in Wisconsin, and it tells the story from the first-person perspective. When an author like Laura Ingalls Wilder writes in first-person, it's as if she is talking right to you. In first-person, the narrator uses the pronouns "I" and "me" instead of "she" or "her" when talking about the main character.

Laura Ingalls Wilder finished the last book in the series in 1943. She was 76 years old. Laura Ingalls Wilder died in 1957. Her books and her childhood live on.

Answer the following questions about the story "Laura Ingalls Wilder." The weights show you how hard you will need to work to find each answer.

1. According to the article, you can infer that life in the 1880s was both

    Ⓐ fun and exciting.   Ⓒ difficult and sweet.

    Ⓑ boring and deadly.   Ⓓ easy and relaxing.

2. In what year was Laura Ingalls Wilder born?

    Ⓐ 1943   Ⓑ 1887   Ⓒ 1957   Ⓓ 1869

3. Which of these sentences is written using the first-person perspective?

    Ⓐ He ate a sandwich, a bag of carrots, and two cookies for lunch.

    Ⓑ You should pack a heavy jacket for your camping trip.

    Ⓒ They have lived next door to her for over 10 years.

    Ⓓ Mom handed me the dishes, and I put them on the table.

4. What was one reason given for why the Ingalls family moved so much?

    Ⓐ The crops failed.

    Ⓑ They didn't like the people.

    Ⓒ They wanted to live where it was cooler.

    Ⓓ The land was too muddy.

On the lines below, write your own question based on "Laura Ingalls Wilder." Circle the correct picture on the left to show the level of the question you wrote.

_____

_____

_____

_____

On a separate piece of paper . . .

- Write a sentence that includes the word *eventually*.

- Can you think of a time in your life that could be made into a story? Make a list of memories you have of your early childhood. Which of the moments on your list can you make into its own story?

The Superpowers of Stan Lee

Spiderman is a teenager with web-slinging powers. The Hulk is a big green guy with anger-management issues. The X-Men are a group of students with special abilities.

What do all of these characters have in common? Their powers set them apart from other humans, and they all came from the mind of one man: Stan Lee.

Stan Lee was born in 1922 in New York City. It was the time of the Great Depression. Many people then were out of work and struggling to make a living. This struggle helped Stanley develop his work ethic. He knew that one needed to work hard in life. In 1939, he worked as an assistant at Timely Comics. He became one of their editors. Timely Comics would eventually change their name to Marvel Comics. Stan Lieber would also change his name to Stan Lee.

Meanwhile, a competing company known as DC had begun developing a group of superheroes called The Justice League. Stan Lee's boss asked if he could create a group of superheroes, too. Lee worked with illustrator Jack Kirby. They created The Fantastic Four. Lee was influenced by science fiction writers like Jules Verne. Quickly, the popularity of The Fantastic Four comic skyrocketed! As a result, Lee was given the go-ahead to create more characters and comics.

Stan Lee's characters may have had superpowers, but they were still very real. His characters were superhuman. They were also very human. They had human flaws. They weren't perfect. They lived with human problems. In fact, some of the issues going on in Stan Lee's own world of the 1960s could be read in the comics he wrote. It was very courageous, for instance, when he had the X-Men take on the topics of racism and prejudice.

Many of Stan Lee's comics were turned into movies and TV shows. In 2008, he received the Medal of Arts award for his innovative contributions. Even the earliest of Stan Lee's characters are still seen on bookshelves, movie theaters, costume stores, and billboards. To this day, he is still creating.

Answer the following questions about the story "The Superpowers of Stan Lee." The weights show you how hard you will need to work to find each answer.

1. In what year was Stan Lee born?

Ⓐ 1960   Ⓒ 1922

Ⓑ 1939   Ⓓ 2008

2. Which of the following superheroes was not created by Stan Lee?

Ⓐ The Hulk   Ⓒ Spiderman

Ⓑ Superman   Ⓓ The X-Men

3. Based on the story, what seems to be the meaning of the word *flaws*?

Ⓐ perfect traits   Ⓒ superpowers

Ⓑ weaknesses   Ⓓ strong points

4. Based on the story, what might the author say is Stan's most impressive superpower?

Ⓐ the ability to have flaws

Ⓑ the ability to edit comic books

Ⓒ the ability to change his name

Ⓓ the ability to create superheroes

On the lines below, write your own question based on "The Superpowers of Stan Lee." Circle the correct picture on the left to show the level of the question you wrote.

_____

_____

_____

_____

_____

On a separate piece of paper . . .

- Write a sentence that includes the word *develop*.

- What superpower would you have if you could? What would be your superhero name?

Worth the Risk?

Would you ever eat something that could make you sick or even kill you? For most people, their answer would be, "Of course not!" For others, there is one fish that is worth the risk, and it is called *fugu*.

Fugu is the Japanese name for the blowfish. Some parts of the blowfish are so poisonous, that they can kill anyone who eats them. The blowfish's liver is particularly dangerous. For this reason, it has been illegal since 1984 to serve the fugu's liver in a restaurant in Japan. Yet, the liver is considered by many to be a delicacy. This means that people think it is a special treat. They are willing to pay lots of money and risk their lives to taste it.

Chefs who safely prepare fugu in restaurants must possess great skill and special equipment. A fugu chef uses a knife with a long, very thin blade to slice the safe parts of the fish away from the unsafe parts. The poisoned parts must not touch the safe parts, or else they will contaminate them. They will transfer the poison onto those parts and make them unsafe to touch or eat.

As a result, being a fugu chef in Japan can be a dangerous occupation. It is also a very high honor. In order to even be allowed to do this job, a chef must complete a tough training process. He or she must spend three years learning how to slice the fish correctly. The chef must then demonstrate this knowledge by taking tests. Fewer than half are able to pass the tests. At the end of training, the chefs take the ultimate exam: they must prepare a plate of fugu and eat it. Some chefs die while taking this test!

So what does a dish of this dangerous delicacy look and taste like? Fugu is usually served raw. (Cooking it would not destroy the poison anyway.) It is usually sliced so thin and so delicately, that you can almost see right through the pieces! These extremely thin pieces are then arranged in artistic patterns on attractive plates. As for the taste, some people consider fugu to be supremely delicious. Others don't think it's that tasty at all. The Emperor of Japan might not know; it is the one food that by law he is not allowed to eat.

Answer the following questions about the story "Worth the Risk?" The weights show you how hard you will need to work to find each answer.

1. Based on the how the word is used in the story, which of the following things would most likely be called *a delicacy*?

    Ⓐ tuna in a can   Ⓒ a rare mushroom

    Ⓑ a burger from a fast-food restaurant   Ⓓ a piece of wheat bread

2. Which of the following is not a way to ensure that a piece of blowfish is safe to eat?

    Ⓐ cooking it for a long time

    Ⓑ slicing it correctly

    Ⓒ having a trained chef prepare it

    Ⓓ keeping it away from contaminated parts

3. According to the story, which part of the blowfish is extremely dangerous?

    Ⓐ the eyes   Ⓑ the fins   Ⓒ the heart   Ⓓ the liver

4. What is the final test a fugu chef must take in order to complete his or her training?

    Ⓐ serving fugu to the Emperor of Japan

    Ⓑ serving a safe dish of fugu liver

    Ⓒ eating fugu he or she has prepared

    Ⓓ sharpening a fugu knife correctly

On the lines below, write your own question based on "Worth the Risk?" Circle the correct picture on the left to show the level of the question you wrote.

_____

_____

_____

_____

On a separate piece of paper . . .

- Write a sentence that includes the word *risk*.

- Do you agree with the law that says the Emperor of Japan cannot eat fugu? Explain your answer.

Selling Made Easy

Most of us have bought something from a vending machine at some point. These convenient machines offer quick and easy snacks and beverages for a fairly low price. But while we may think of chips and candy and soda when we hear the words "vending machine," these devices have always dispensed more than just food.

So how did vending machines begin? The modern vending machine was first put into use in London, England. This happened in the early 1880s. That first machine sold postcards. The first machine put into use in the United States sold packs of gum in New York City. This happened in 1888. Since then, vending machines have been used more and more. Here are some important milestones that vending machines achieved during the 20th century.

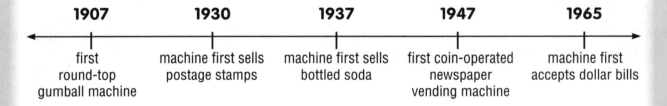

1907	1930	1937	1947	1965
first round-top gumball machine	machine first sells postage stamps	machine first sells bottled soda	first coin-operated newspaper vending machine	machine first accepts dollar bills

Today's vending machines can give out everything from mobile phones to bicycles. And the food that these machines give out is not simply chips and candy and soda. Some dispense meat, raw eggs, or freshly baked pizza. There is even a vending machine in Maine where customers can use a claw to pick out a live lobster.

Where will vending machines go from here? Their future is most likely bright. They are convenient to use and cheap to operate. Vending-machine owners do not have to pay employees to work them. They can be open 24 hours a day, 7 days a week.

Answer the following questions about the story "Selling Made Easy." The weights show you how hard you will need to work to find each answer.

1. Based on the passage, what does the word *convenient* mean?

(A) cheap   (C) quick and easy

(B) important   (D) modern

2. Which is **not** given as a reason why vending machines may have a bright future?

(A) They are always open.

(B) They are cheap to operate.

(C) People find them convenient to use.

(D) People would rather buy from a machine than a person.

3. According to the timeline, what couldn't vending machines do before 1950?

(A) give you change for a dollar bill

(B) sell you a newspaper

(C) sell you a bottled soda

(D) dispense gumballs

4. About how many years passed between the time when packs of gum were first sold in vending machines in New York and when the first round-top gumball machine was used?

(A) 7 years   (B) 9 years   (C) 19 years   (D) 29 years

On the lines below, write your own question based on "Selling Made Easy." Circle the correct picture on the left to show the level of the question you wrote.

_____

_____

_____

_____

On a separate piece of paper . . .

- Write a sentence that includes the word *dispense*.

- If you could design a vending machine that sold some of your favorite things, what would it sell? Draw a picture of this vending machine.

E-mailing Etiquette

Let's say you went on a weekend trip with your family, and your car broke down. You open up your smartphone and send this e-mail your teacher:

> Sorry Mr. K. i wont b in class Mon 'cuz our car broke down on way home from g-mas hse. LOL! C U Tues!

Texting is the way that many students communicate these days. However, e-mailing a teacher or coach is different than texting a friend. You need to show good netiquette. The word *netiquette* is made by combing the words *net* and *etiquette*. It's a new word that means, "showing good online manners."

When you are e-mailing someone, you need to be more formal than you would be if you were texting a friend. Use these three simple rules of netiquette:

1. Avoid using texting shorthand. That is, don't use abbreviations like "LOL" or "C U" to communicate words or phrases. If it's important enough to write an e-mail, it's important enough to type whole words.
2. Make sure your conventions are correct. Think about GUMS—Grammar, Usage, Mechanics, and Spelling. Remember that every piece of writing is an assessment. It's a test of how you write and how respectful you are.
3. Use a greeting or an introductory phrase. Also, make sure you sign your e-mail. If you don't type your name at the bottom of the post, then your teacher might not recognize your e-mail address.

If the student had known these three simple rules, the e-mail would have sounded much more professional and impressive. It could have read:

Dear Mr. Kirkpatrick,

I'm sorry I won't be in class on Monday. Unfortunately, our car broke down on the way home from visiting my grandmother's house. I look forward to seeing you on Tuesday. Please let me know what work I missed, and I would be happy to make it up.

Sincerely, Sam

Answer the following questions about the story "E-mailing Etiquette." The weights show you how hard you will need to work to find each answer.

1. If you show good "netiquette," what do you do?

   Ⓐ You fold a net correctly.

   Ⓑ You are polite in the classroom.

   Ⓒ You display respect to those older than you.

   Ⓓ You display good online manners.

2. Based on the passage, which of the following choices is an example of texting shorthand?

   Ⓐ LOL   Ⓒ IDK

   Ⓑ CU   Ⓓ all of the above

3. Fill in the blank: You need to use correct _____ when e-mailing.

   Ⓐ abbreviations   Ⓒ texting

   Ⓑ conventions   Ⓓ sketching

4. Based on how the word is used in the story, which of the following is an assessment?

   Ⓐ a piece of mail   Ⓒ a written letter

   Ⓑ a lesson   Ⓓ a test

On the lines below, write your own question based on "E-mailing Etiquette." Circle the correct picture on the left to show the level of the question you wrote.

_____

_____

_____

_____

On a separate piece of paper . . .

- Write a sentence that includes the word *netiquette.*

- Write a 2–3 sentence e-mail using texting. Then, pass it to your classmate and have him or her translate it into a more professional e-mail. You translate the one he or she passes to you.

Translating Thoughts Into Words

People once used quill pens to write letters. They even sent messages using Morse code. Then, in 1808, Christopher Latham Sholes invented the typewriter. The typewriter had a board with keys representing different letters and numbers. Much like a piano player can hit a key and that key strikes a note, a person can use the keys on a typewriter to create words on a page.

Here is how a typewriter works:

1. The user pushes down on a key that has a letter or punctuation mark.

2. Inside the typewriter, a little hammer with the letter on it strikes a ribbon with ink on it.

3. Behind the ink ribbon is the piece of paper that will contain the finished product. The letter shape is pressed in ink onto the paper.

The board of keys on a typewriter works almost the same as computer keyboards do today. However, today's keyboards are digital input devices. They put information into another device. Each key is a broken circuit. Imagine a circle of energy. The circle is connected, and the energy travels all along the ring. But if you cut the circle, the energy can't travel all around the circle. A key on a keyboard is like that. When you tap it, it closes the circle of energy. By tapping the key—let's say the letter "B"—a user completes the circuit. A signal is sent that represents that letter. Next, the computer translates that signal to the screen. The computer looks up the signal in a kind of dictionary called a computer map. Then, out pops a "B" on the monitor. The character map also translates combinations of keys. If you hold down the "Shift" key and the "1" key, out pops an exclamation mark.

A keyboard is an amazing translator. It translates what you click into what you see.

Answer the following questions about the story "Translating Thoughts Into Words." The weights show you how hard you will need to work to find each answer.

1. In what year was the typewriter invented?

   Ⓐ 1888   Ⓑ 1808   Ⓒ 1018   Ⓓ 1088

2. What simile is used to help describe the actions of the typewriter's keyboard?

   Ⓐ A keyboard is compared to a piano.
   Ⓑ A keyboard is compared to a finger.
   Ⓒ A keyboard is compared to a circuit.
   Ⓓ A keyboard is compared to a tile.

3. To what does the author compare a key on a keyboard?

   Ⓐ It is like a dictionary that translates the keys to letters on the screen.
   Ⓑ It is like a hammer that hits the letters onto the screen.
   Ⓒ It is like a circuit that sends a signal to the computer.
   Ⓓ It is like a bolt of energy that zaps the letter onto the page.

4. According to the passage, what have people used to write down their thoughts?

   Ⓐ quill pens   Ⓒ Morse code
   Ⓑ typewriters   Ⓓ all of the above

On the lines below, write your own question based on "Translating Thoughts Into Words." Circle the correct picture on the left to show the level of the question you wrote.

_____

_____

_____

_____

On a separate piece of paper . . .

- Write a sentence that includes the word *translate*.

- Look at the top row of a keyboard. The letters are Q, W, E, R, T, Y, U, I, O, and P. How many words can you create from those letters in five minutes? Make a list.

Speaking Without Fear

Did you know that one of the leading phobias in the country is speaking in front of a group? It's called *glossophobia*, and it affects many people. A *phobia* is something you are scared of. More than almost any other phobia, people are afraid of public speaking.

But that does not have to be the case for everyone. There are some steps you can take to help you be prepared when you speak in front of people. These steps will help you speak better. In addition, with good preparation, following these rules should make you less nervous.

Here are things to think about when presenting in front of a group:

- **Volume** — Make sure the back of the room can hear you. Sometimes it helps to focus on a point—for example, a poster—in the back of the room and speak to that point.

- **Posture** — Stand up straight. Don't slouch. Put your shoulders back.

- **Speed** — Don't go so fast that people can't understand you. Remember, you think you sound slower than you actually do, so don't be scared to slow it down.

- **Eye Contact** — Make sure you are looking at people. Don't look at the ground or the ceiling for the words. Look at actual people. Also, don't focus on just one person. Your eyes should travel to other people in the room.

- **Gestures** — Use gestures to highlight your points, but don't show your nerves in your gestures. Don't fidget or rock back and forth. Stay calm and use gestures that are needed. Be in control of them.

- **Be Prepared** — Write the piece you are going to be talking about ahead of time. This will give you time to rehearse it, time it, and perfect it.

The key is to practice. Nobody speaks well who doesn't speak at all. Push yourself to raise your hand in class. Ask questions and offer answers. Get your voice out there regularly, and you won't be so frightened to present occasionally.

Answer the following questions about the story "Speaking Without Fear." The weights show you how hard you will need to work to find each answer.

1. Based on what you learned from the story, what can you infer is the meaning of *arithmophobia*?

Ⓐ fear of public speaking   Ⓒ love of math
Ⓑ fear of math   Ⓓ presenting in public

2. What is one way you can show good posture?

Ⓐ by looking all around the room   Ⓒ by putting your shoulders back
Ⓑ by rocking back and forth   Ⓓ by raising your voice

3. According to the article, which of the following is **not** something you need to think about when giving an oral presentation?

Ⓐ using good volume
Ⓑ being prepared ahead of time
Ⓒ making sure you aren't going too fast
Ⓓ making sure your audience agrees with you

4. According to the passage, when should gestures be used?

Ⓐ all the time, with every word   Ⓒ to wave to the audience
Ⓑ to highlight some important points   Ⓓ rarely

On the lines below, write your own question based on "Speaking Without Fear." Circle the correct picture on the left to show the level of the question you wrote.

_____
_____
_____
_____

On a separate piece of paper . . .

• Write a sentence that includes the word *offer*.

• Write a short paragraph about your favorite hobby. Memorize it and present it to your class. Try to use the advice given in the article.

Answer Key

Accept appropriate responses for the final three entries on the question-and-answer pages.

What Is a Geode? (page 11)
1. C   3. D
2. A   4. C

One Final Flight (page 13)
1. A   3. D
2. D   4. A

An Eye for Color (page 15)
1. B   3. D
2. A   4. A

The Magical Möbius Strip (page 17)
1. D   3. D
2. C   4. A

The Five Most Deadly Sharks (page 19)
1. B   3. D
2. C   4. A

Unsung Heroes (page 21)
1. D   3. D
2. B   4. B

Hamilton vs. Burr (page 23)
1. A   3. A
2. D   4. C

A New Kind of Treasure Hunt (page 25)
1. B   3. A
2. C   4. D

Record-Breaking Mountains (page 27)
1. C   3. D
2. C   4. A

A Famous Face (page 29)
1. B   3. D
2. B   4. D

The Blue Jean King (page 31)
1. A   3. A
2. C   4. D

Mario Batali (page 33)
1. D   3. C
2. B   4. C

Laura Ingalls Wilder (page 35)
1. C   3. D
2. D   4. A

The Superpowers of Stan Lee (page 37)
1. C   3. B
2. B   4. D

Worth the Risk? (page 39)
1. C   3. D
2. A   4. C

Selling Made Easy (page 41)
1. C   3. A
2. D   4. C

E-mailing Etiquette (page 43)
1. D   3. B
2. D   4. D

Translating Thoughts Into Words (page 45)
1. B   3. C
2. A   4. D

Speaking Without Fear (page 47)
1. B   3. D
2. C   4. B